the WORKBOOK
HEALING THROUGH ART

■

the companion to

TENDING TO MY WOUNDS
Coping with Grief One Square at a Time

Debra Smelik Walling

ISBN : 978-0-9962010-5-6

www.dswalling.com

the WORKBOOK
HEALING THROUGH ART

At the temple, there is a poem called "Loss" carved into the stone.
It has three words but the poet has scratched them out.
You cannot read Loss… only feel it.

Arthur Golden

TABLE OF CONTENTS

Greetings --- 1

Types of Loss --- 3

Healing Through Art --- 5

Common Emotions and Stages --- 7

A Story to Tell --- 9

Types of Support --- 11

Let's Get Started --- 13

Step-by-Step One: Make a Commitment --- 14

                      My Commitment --- 15

Step-by-StepTwo: Canvas Type and Size --- 16

Step-by-Step Three: Pencil, Eraser and Ruler --- 17

Step-by-Step Four: Grid the Canvas --- 18

Workbook Example: Steps One through Four --- 19

Step-by-Step Five: Ink in the Grid --- 21

Step-by-Step Six: Timer. Ready, Set, Draw --- 22

Workbook Example: Steps Five and Six --- 23

Step-by-Step Seven: Repeat. Ready, Set, Draw --- 24

Workbook Example: Step Seven --- 25

Step-by-Step Eight: Optional, Background Color --- 26

Workbook Example: Step Eight --- 27

Step-by-Step Nine: Optional, Adding Color --- 28

Workbook Example: Step Nine --- 29

Overview --- 30

List of Supplies --- 31

Books Help Heal --- 32

In Closing --- 33

Blank Pages --- 34

Do not go where the path may lead, go instead
where there is no path and leave a trail.

Ralph Waldo Emerson

GREETINGS

When disheartened by the great sadness from a loss or anything that needs to be healed in our lives, words may no longer be enough to help us recover from the pain of grief. Beyond words, this workbook aids in renewing the spirit using creativity and self-expression to help tap into our innate creativity.

A companion to my book *Tending To My Wounds, Coping With Grief One Square at a Time*, this workbook instructs and guides one through the art process used in the book, an example of how healing through art can be beneficial as one paves the path to self-discovery, self-healing. It suggests a simple exercise that helped me learn to refocus after a loss. Perhaps this workbook may do the same for you.

> **There is a restorative power in healing through art that cannot be discovered until we dare to venture. It is a safe place to participate in our own recovery.**

This workbook is a step-by-step guide with examples. Blank pages are provided at the end of the workbook to get you started in creating your own square-a-day with words to inspire and hopefully stimulate the creativity of your heart.

My journey through grief began with the written expression of my grief; journaling thoughts, prayers or poetry that unexpectedly and abruptly surfaced. Too, when surrounded by those who also grieve, like my dad, sister and brother, I found attentive listening to be limited; therefore, writing became my place for solace, a place to retreat. Beyond the aid from support groups, self-help books, conversations, prayers, and even journaling I found myself still searching for yet another avenue to help put closure on my grief.

The square-a-day visual expression of my grief emerged one year following my mother's death. Titled Project SaD (square-a-day) because at the time of my mother's death, that is what I was - sad. *Tending to My Wounds, Coping with Grief One Square at a Time* holds the canvas images of Project SaD, the visual expressions of my grief with journal entries, the written expressions of my grief. Both separate journeys all their own. Joining the two, a third journey evolved and where I chose to put closure on my grief.

To grieve, mourn and bereave a loss, the experience varies greatly from one person to the next. What works for some may or may not work for others. We do not know what heals until explored. It is my hope as you seek a peaceful heart in times of darkness, this workbook will encourage and possibly put you a step closer to finding some comfort or even closure in your grief.

THOUGHTS, NOTES OR DOODLES

_____

_____

_____

_____

_____

Grief never ends, but it changes. It is a passage, not a place to stay. The sense of loss
must give way if we are to value the life that was lived.

Author Unknown

Loss is a human experience we will encounter at some point in our life and we will experience grief. A time of difficulty and struggle, loss of any kind causes mental or emotional stress. Grief has a pervasive impact on our psyche and can become an obstacle while we maintain that sense of oneness.

In order to journey through grief with any hope of healing, to adjust and begin life anew, it is important to recognize your grief, value it and accept it.

- Death of a Person or a Pet
- Loss of a House
- Miscarriage
- Loss of a Job
- Divorce, Relationship Breakup
- Loss of Friendship
- Retirement
- Loss of Trust in God or Parent

What type of loss are you experiencing?
Is your loss current, recent or one from long ago?

Either I will find a way or I will make one.

Philip Sidney

HEALING THROUGH ART

Typically in an art therapy session, the chosen form of art created would be reviewed by an Art Therapist. Trained to recognize nonverbal symbols and metaphors that can be revealed in a visual expression, the Art Therapist can help the client understand what would have otherwise been difficult, perhaps awkwardly written or verbalized words. The thoughts or feelings being communicated in the art can therefore help one gain insight, to possibly obtain a better understanding of oneself or the relationship with others.

> **The healing through art journey described within this workbook is my self-guided therapy. A solo journey with no one to review, criticize my grief or take a peek unless I wanted to open that part of my grief to others.**

When a therapeutic art form was suggested as an avenue to venture on my own, there would not be an Art Therapist to examine or review. No one to study or reveal the message held deep within this practice. It was not what might be revealed for I already knew my psyche was askew. I already knew I was depressed, sad, lonely, and missing my mom. More so, it was the importance to begin the suggested exercise in hope of two things. After all, grief projects a behavior and we need to refocus on something other then the pain.

First, I thought the task of and the commitment to one small square-a-day would help me refocus after my loss. Grief has a way of muddling the mind, causing behavior to surprise not only yourself but those around you. This provided the opportunity to realize it was time to quit floundering and instead make some type of commitment in starting to reclaim my life.

Second, the endeavor offered the possibility of another escape to a special place. There I could relieve some of the grief, sadness and sorrow that sporadically continued to blanket my soul, those thoughts and feelings unable to put into words. A place where I could share with others, only if I so desired.

In art therapy, evidence-based research indicates the process of creation is to improve mental health and to maintain emotional well-being.

Looking back I realize the impact of a doctor's suggestion as I mourned the death of my mother. What I discovered was recovery through this somewhat meditative state engaging the visual journaling of my emotions. Instead of words, I used shapes, color, memories, and moments of the past and the present to tend to my wounded spirit— passing through the suffering and returning to the land of the living.

_____

_____

_____

_____

_____

_____

Goodbyes are only for those who love with their eyes.
Because for those who love with heart and soul, there is no separation.

Rumi

The journey through grief may be short-lived and respectful, allowing a peaceful calm where life after death is more easily adjusted. Yet the experience for some might be seemingly endless and way more difficult to process. When grief becomes unbearable, weighing heavily on the mind and exhausting the spirit, mental health counseling or art therapy is frequently recommended.

Either way, while experiencing great sadness a myriad of physical, mental and emotional symptoms or stages will occur. In varying degrees and in no particular order; grief has no timetable and no set standards of severity. At some point we will meet the emotions and stages of grief.

They may hit all at once, sometimes not at all. They can loop back and forth and sometimes hit with a completely different set of physical, emotional and mental symptoms. Do not dismiss a single one for they are normal. Grief occurs and when it does, allow grief the time it needs. Below are the emotions and stages I personally experienced. Based on grief resources including those by Elisabeth Kübler-Ross, my emotions and stages are quite common and natural.

- Denial, Shock
- Resentment, Guilt
- Isolation, Despondency, Depression
- Lack of Energy
- Feeling Lost, Disoriented, Emptiness
- Forgetfulness, Lack of Motivation
- Preoccupied, Indecisiveness
- Withdrawal
- Pain
- Lack of Productivity
- Bargaining
- Acceptance
- Insomnia, Headaches, Clumsiness
- Apathy

What stages and symptoms manifested in your sadness?

Let me not pray to be sheltered from dangers,
but to be fearless in facing them.
Let me not beg for the stilling of my pain,
but for the heart to conquer it.

Rabindranath Tagore

A STORY TO TELL

We all have a story to tell. Do not ignore your feelings. Recognize them, accept them and value them. Sharing your story of the loss you are experiencing or the life and death of your loved one is significant.

Telling the story is what helps us to heal.
This visual creation is all about you. Create your own calm.

Our story is usually shared in a group, over the phone or face-to-face with a family member, friend or mentor. When support systems or resources no longer provide the care and support wanted or needed, do no be afraid to venture on your own. You may very well find solitude provides the type of support you need. Too, what we want or need as we grieve may not always be readily accessible or obtainable. Therefore, the reason to search for alternative sources is to help us through as we create our own haven for healing.

In grief we need an outlet for expressing emotions; the outlet is personal and it needs to happen.

The commitment to creating your own square-a-day, is a solo journey free from platitudes and attitudes, free of the 'you should have' from others. It is non-verbal—the telling of your story based on your own terms and shared only if you choose to do so.

No matter the type of loss experienced, how you feel, handle and contend with the difficulties of loss it is truly a distinctive and personal journey that will be expressed and experienced in ways so very different from one person to the next.

As a guide, the instructions in this workbook are about how and what I used to tell my story creating the art in Tending To My Wounds, Coping with Grief One Square at a Time.

The art you are about to create is the telling of your story. It is personal. The process is about what feels good to you, what medium is comfortable and most accessible to you.

Fill the paper with the breathings of
your own heart.

William Wordsworth

_____

_____

_____

_____

_____

_____

Should you shield the valleys from the windstorms,
you would never see the beauty of their canyons.

Elisabeth Kübler-Ross

Time moves differently for those who grieve, mourn or bereave. The approach to healing starts with acknowledging the loss and accepting the sadness and its pain. Though crucial, this can be difficult to do. Grief can be a lonely experience and quite challenging.

Rebuilding perspective is very important and a positive step is to surround yourself with supportive people and resources. The circle needs to consist of caring and encouraging people you can trust, who will listen openly and provide emotional and possible physical support.

- Family, Friends
- Colleagues, Co-Workers
- Grief Counselor, Therapist
- Support Groups
- Self-Help, Self-Care
- Clergy, Church Family

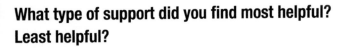

What type of support did you find most helpful?
Least helpful?

11

A failure is not always a mistake. It may simply be the best one you can do under the circumstances. The real mistake is to stop trying.

B. F. Skinner

The following **Step-By-Step Instructions and Illustrations** will guide you to create a square-a-day canvas based on the process used to produce the art canvases in Project SaD. Whether you use the blank pages provided at the end of this workbook or work directly on a canvas of your choice, you will be ready to start creating your art, your way.

LET'S GET STARTED

Life becomes uprooted when loss occurs. Emotionally numb, we can get forced down into the depths of despair. Our psyche is damaged making it difficult to get back on track; a roller coaster of emotions that constantly get in the way of healing.

Staying focused as we walk through grief can be one of the most difficult things to do.

Having a daily goal helps. Setting and keeping one small goal is a stepping stone to help regain momentum in life after a loss. One way to get back on track, helping us to revive and heal the soul and the spirit is with the self-expression and self-discovery found in art.

Remind yourself the process is not to see what you can or cannot draw. What is important is the intention behind this exercise —

- Encourage a new behavior to help shift the grieving heart from the distractions that muddle the mind, those that cause us to lose focus, become absent-minded and unable to complete set goals.
- Healing through art: setting a goal, committing to that goal and allowing the pain and sadness of your grief to be your teacher.

THE PROCESS

Creating a visual of our grief by filling in one square within the allotted time of 15 minutes, per day for the committed number of days with the option of adding color using only three colors. Why the restrictions? Because in grief the mind is already strained and there is the tendency to overthink our thoughts, our actions, our behaviors. The purpose here is not to think but instead, to quickly release what we are feeling on our chosen canvas. With few options keeps the task simple while allowing us to stay focused on the task at hand.

The intention of this exercise may not heal you 100% from your grief though is a diversion that just might put you one step closer to heal, to carry on, to better focus as you learn to live life without the loss you experienced.

STEP-BY-STEP ONE

One way to help refocus after a loss, **Make A Commitment** to redirect your grief by giving it a visual through art expression. The commitment is for one of the following:

- One Day = 1 square
- One Week = 7 squares
- One Month = 28, 30 or 31 squares
- One Year = 365 squares

Daily you will be timed for 15 minutes, filling in one square per day until the end of the committed number of days. Determine the number of day(s) you will commit to and base your decision on what you KNOW you will complete. It is not the length of the commitment that is important; it is the keeping of that commitment.

**The example in this workbook is based on one week;
a commitment to seven days, seven squares.**

CHOICES I MADE

I committed to one month.   My starting date was in February. Consisting of 28 days meant I committed to 28 squares. The plan was to stop at month's end. I did not. Nineteen grief canvases followed.

I continue the practice today not because of grief. It is my place to release any stress or joy, maintain a good attitude and enhance well-being through this somewhat meditative practice.

When patterns are broken,
new worlds emerge.

Tufi Kupferberg

I, _____, will carry out the Healing Through Art exercise explained in this workbook with the intent to work towards bringing balance back into my life. To help recapture the joy in life after the loss I experienced.

I understand this to be an exercise in self-expression producing a visual of my thoughts and feelings. I am ready to reconnect with myself and my life by looking inward — to allow my heart to see the beacon of light that does shine within while my hand guides me through my sadness and sorrow —one square at a time.

By using the blank pages at the end of this workbook or with a different type of canvas, I will commit to:

Please check one:

☐ One Day = 1 square
☐ One Week - 7 square
☐ One Month = 28, 30 or 31 days
☐ One Year = 365 days

_____

Signature   Date

There's a difference between interest and commitment. When you're interested in doing something, you do it only when it's convenient. When you're committed to something, you accept no excuses - only results.

Kenneth Blanchard

STEP-BY-STEP TWO

Select a Canvas Type and Size

The choice of canvas and the desired size will depend on your style, your mood or even your budget. Canvas types can be whatever your creative mind comes up with. Consider the following:

- All purpose drawing paper, like Bristol, charcoal, pastel or watercolor papers
- Index Card
- Art Canvas
- Copier Paper
- Journal
- Cloth
- Board

CHOICES I MADE

Canvas Type and Size: A gallery-wrapped canvas because it does not have any visible nails or staples holding the canvas to the stretchers on the sides. The edges of a gallery-wrap canvas are often painted a neutral color and once the piece is complete it is suitable to be hung without a frame. Chosen size, a 16"x20". My intention, to do only one canvas. I thought that was all I needed or wanted to do. At the end of the month I was compelled to continue the committed process. Sizes ranged from 5"x5" up to 40"x40". Recently I added the use of paper, wood and testing out the possibilities of using discarded paintings.

STEP-BY-STEP THREE

Pencil, Eraser and Ruler

Depending on your skill level and canvas choice you might prefer exploring and using other pencil types. However for this exercise, a standard school grade No. 2 pencil will do the trick and is used to grid the canvas and draw. I found the eraser at the end of the pencil was not enough. Erasers to consider are pink pearl, white vinyl, vanish 4-in-1 or the kneaded eraser. It's a matter of preference and what works for you and the type of canvas. The ruler comes in handy for obtaining straight grid lines. A metal, wooden or plastic ruler will suit just fine. As for the ruler length, again a matter of preference, what you might have on hand or the size of your canvas.

CHOICES I MADE

Pencil: A standard school grade No. 2 pencil though found if pressed too hard when drawing it was difficult to erase in its entirety. I had to relax a little and ease up on the amount of pressure used. Eraser: I tried a lot, a Vanish 4-in-1 eraser worked best for me. Ruler: an 18" metal ruler and a T-square for drawing right angles, though not necessary. It was available so I used it. I opted to use items found around the house and to keep the cost down.

STEP-BY-STEP FOUR

Grid the Canvas

Once the canvas is selected, with pencil and the aid of a ruler lightly grid the canvas into a series of squares according to the number of committed days.

One Day = 1 square
One Week = 7 squares
One Month = 28, 30 or 31 squares
One Year = 365 squares

Depending on the canvas size a perfect square will not always be possible; rectangles, even circles or a combination of might need to be your choice in order to grid the canvas to the number of committed days.

God turns you from one feeling to another and teaches you by means of opposites,
so that you will have two wings to fly, not one.

Rumi

WORKBOOK EXAMPLE

STEPS ONE THROUGH FOUR

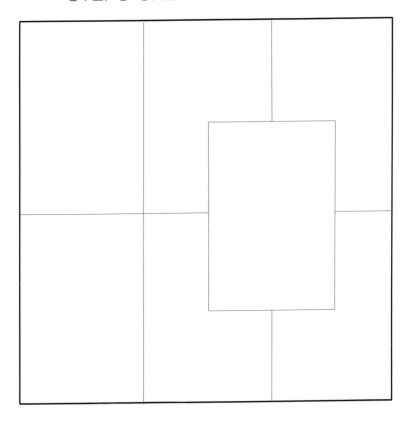

STEP-BY-STEP FIVE

Ink in the Grid

Once the canvas is gridded into the committed number of squares, go over the pencil marks with a permanent marker. The reason — to prevent the urge of wanting to go back and change, correct or start over.

Sharpie permanent marker, black, fine point

Immediately ink in the pencil grid lines. When dry, erase any visible pencil markings that might remain. The Sharpie will also be used after each pencil drawn square.

Let the drawing begin...

From this point onward you will begin filling in the gridded squares on your canvas - one square at a time, one day at a time.

REMINDER

Making a perfect drawing is not what this exercise is about.
It is about spontaneity in releasing a thought or emotion within the time limit.

A creative thought at first seems ridiculous and unimportant, an increase in those who cherish it assures that hiding your creativity hides you for the rest of your life.

Michael B. Johnson

STEP-BY-STEP SIX

Timer

Be it the timer on a cell phone, an alarm clock, a sand timer, or an egg timer this is needed to make certain you draw within the allotted time only. If you do not think you need one, reconsider. The allotted time of 15 minutes is not a lot of time, especially if drawing techniques and talents at the novice level. Without setting a timer I became distracted, constantly looking at the clock to make certain I did not go over the allotted time. A timer allowed me to stay focused on my drawing and not the time.

Ready, Set, Draw

Timer set? Pick only one square, any square* and start drawing. Fill in the square with whatever the hand and mind lead you to draw: a shape, a doddle, an image, a scribble, words, a symbol, a line, a dot. What is your heart telling you to draw? Erase if need be and draw some more. When timer alarms, STOP – immediately ink in what was drawn using the Sharpie mentioned in Step 5. Do not make changes, additional or deletions. Ink in what was originally drawn. Use eraser to remove any visible pencil marks that remain. That is it for the day. Set canvas aside until the next day.

*Optional : On the backside of the canvas and with a light touch of the pencil, I chose to number my squares on the day they were completed. Most of my canvases are for 1 month. On the backside each square was numbered according to the day it was drawn.

CHOICES I MADE

My approach to each chosen square was based on my mood. Just as I allowed the hand to move across the canvas so did I let the hand lead me to what square would be filled on that particular day.

STEPS FIVE AND SIX

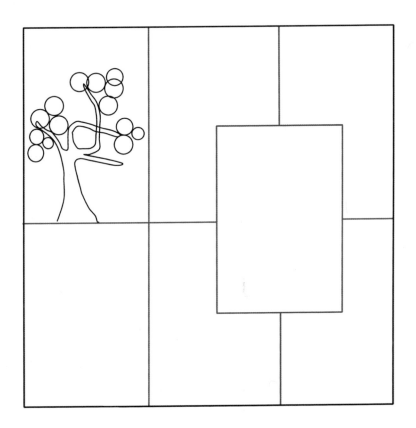

REPEAT
Ready, Set, Draw

Each day return to the canvas.

1. Pick one square.
2. Set timer for 15 minutes.
3. Draw. Erase if necessary and continue drawing.
4. When timer alarms, STOP!
5. Ink in what was drawn, using the Sharpie. Allow to dry and erase any visible pencil marks that remain.
6. On backside of canvas note the day (optional).
7. Set canvas aside.
8. Repeat this process each day until the entire canvas is filled.

REMINDER

Grief generates a behavior that may or may not alter the mind immediately. Yet when struck with the sadness of grief, we do take on a behavior that changes our outlook. Our point of view or general attitude to life changes making it difficult to focus.

Remind yourself the purpose behind this exercise is the self-expression of your grief sadness through art. It may not heal you 100% from your grief though it is a diversion. One that just might put you a step closer to healing, to carry on, to better focus as you learn to live life without the loss you experienced, or possibly put closure on your grief.

STEP SEVEN

STEP-BY-STEP EIGHT, OPTIONAL

Background Color for Canvas

In general, most types of canvas will have a white background.

- Will you keep the background as is?
- Do you prefer color?

Now is the time to add color using the appropriate medium for the type of canvas chosen. If a background color is your choice, once painted do allow drying time before proceeding. Depending on your background choice of color to be transparent or more opaque, remember to keep the grid lines visible.

**Life is brighter when the mind is open and even more so when splashed with color.
What color is your humor, rage, funk, or groove?**

CHOICES I MADE

The background on some of my canvases were left as purchased for my mood wanted a white background while other canvases were given a background color. The color choice varied, also depending on my mood. While attempting to keep my cost down I rummaged through the used interior latex paint cans at home. For a background color I made a latex wash, thinning down the water-based latex paint with water (2 parts paint to 1 part water). Once blended I painted the canvas with the wash and immediately ragged it off leaving a semi-opaque, hint of color.

STEP EIGHT

Adding Color to the Squares

With all squares on the canvas filled, step back and take a look at your creation. Will you choose to add color in part or all? Possibly, if you chose not to paint the canvas background as indicated above you might also prefer the absence of color for the drawn images. The understated elegance found in black and white is quite a stylish appearance. However, if a splash of color is preferred, allow **only three colors** to used to fill in part or all of your drawn images.

Why just three colors? Simplicity. When allowing too many colors choices we are prone to ponder, losing focus that will eventually require more time and effort. Anxiety and high expectations might surface leading one to self-blame if the choices do not work out. Using three colors also allows us to be more creative and the purpose of this exercise is to help us become more focused.

Medium of Choice and Paint Brushes

Consideration must be given based on your choice of canvas. Depending on your canvas the possibilities for a medium of choice might be watercolor, oils, colored pencil, markers, or acrylic paint. Unless one has a watercolor canvas most any kind of paints can be used for an art canvas.

Paint brushes used are also based on your choice of canvas. They come in a variety of sizes and the size depends on what best suits your canvas type, your style. Throughout this entire process the paint brushes are the only item that I went out of my way to use a better quality. I noticed a world of difference in less expensive paint brushes to the slightly more expensive ones when it came time to paint what was drawn; same applies to colored pencils.

CHOICES I MADE

Same applies as the background color choice. To keep the cost down I used what was available to me, in my case - the of three colors came from discarded interior latex house paint.

STEP NINE

OVERVIEW

- Commit to a number of days you know you will commit to.
- Select a Canvas Type and Size.
- Grid chosen canvas into number of squares according to committed number of days.
- Ink in grid, allow to dry and erase any visible lines.
- Locate and set a timer for 15 minutes
- Start timer. Pick a square, any square and immediately fill in the square. Draw, doodle or write. DO NOT dwell on what might fill the square, the purpose is to allow your mind, your heart, your hand to lead you. The goal is to fill the space based on your emotions or thoughts, good or bad — whether the space holds something recognizable or not.
- Once the time alarms, STOP! Set the pencil aside and immediately ink in what was drawn. Do not make any changes, additions or deletions. Ink it what was originally drawn. Allow ink to dry and then, if necessary, erase any visible pencil marks that remain.
- Optional: On the backside of canvas, using a pencil and with a light hand, number the square you filled in. e.g. "1" for Day 1, "2" for Day 2, etc.
- Set canvas aside.
- Next day — repeat as shown above until the canvas is completely filled in for chosen number of days.
- When complete, make certain all drawings and grid lines are inked in. Step back to admire your creation. Decide if your canvas will have a background color. If so, add color to accommodate type of canvas used. Allow for drying time before proceeding.
- Will your images remain as is, unpainted or will you add color. If so, use only three colors. as noted on page 28. Get as creative as you want. Remember to use a medium of choice based on your canvas type.
- Step back and admire your competed canvas. Hopefully there was some found therapeutic value in this simple task. The intention of this exercise may not heal you 100% from your grief though is a diversion that just might put you one step closer to heal, to carry on, to better focus as you learn to live life without the loss you experienced.

LIST OF SUPPLIES

A list of basic art supplies is needed to carry out this healing through art exercise. Keep in mind the visual story you are about to tell is all about you; your pain, your sadness, your loss. This is only a guideline to help get you started in creating your own square-a-day canvas. Tap in to your innate creativity by using the supplies that you know will allow you to commit and follow through the exercise until the end.

1. **CANVAS TYPE AND SIZE.** All purpose drawing paper like Bristol, charcoal and pastel papers, Copier Paper, Index Card, Artist Canvas, Journal, Cloth, even Board

2. **PENCIL.** Standard school grade No. 2 pencil

3. **ERASER.** Although the eraser at the tip of your pencil might suffice, other erasers offer better performance such as: Pink Pearl, White Vinyl, Vanish 4-in-1, or kneaded eraser.

4. **RULER.** Not necessary though does help with straight lines and angles. Rulers are available in metal, wooden or plastic.

5. **PERMANENT MARKER.** Black, fine point, Sharpie worked for the art canvases in the book, Tending To My Wounds, Coping with Grief One Square at a Time. Your choice may be different depending on the canvas type being used.

6. **TIMER.** Timer on a cell phone, an alarm clock or an egg timer.

7. **MEDIUM.** Watercolors, Acrylic paints, Pastels, even Colored Pencils.

8. **BRUSHES.** If using paint, size and type of brushes depend on canvas and medium used. A better quality offers a better ending result.

9. **HELP.** Please do not hesitate to contact me should you have any questions or thoughts to share. I would be honored to see what you are working on or hear what you have to say. Visit www.dswalling.com.

Read in their entirety or thumbed through to what piques our interest, books have been a part of healing on many levels. The diverse medley of books available on death, loss and grief each offer some aid to heal. Yet, as unique as grief is to each individual, each book will be equally different as it will be for the individual picking and choosing what might work as they piece their life back together.

When asked what books helped me heal during my grief from death or the loss from three miscarriages, there were many. The majority of my book collection on healing from loss and grief was formed through the love of family, friends and strangers who gave the gift of books. Those that helped in their time of loss or those they felt offered a direct link to my path in finding peace.

There in the written word, pages from books that help heal gave advise, shared experiences and knowledge. Encouragement, inspiration, motivation, and peace could be had, when allowed. A place to cope, instill optimism and even those pages that held imagery surprisingly comforted. Some helped to heal more then others and although I did not find all the answers to my pain and sorrow, the information in books did distract me if only for a short while. Books definitely played a part in my healing and unlike people, books cannot judge.

What works for one does not necessarily work for others. During an exchange of personal experiences and books referenced, a man in his mid 50's shared, "I cannot say I looked for any books to help me with my mother's passing, just tears." A reminder, in loss how muddled the mind becomes, how loss harrows the soul and how very different we are.

Grief, with its unpredictable self, can be challenging and affects our being. Difficult to erase emotional memory, death or any experienced loss changes us to some degree and thereafter determines the quality of our life. We are different.

What Titles that helped you to heal?

Contact Us

- Healing After Loss, Martha Whitmore Hickman
- Prayers for Healing, Conair Press
- No Death, No Fear, Thich Nhat Hahn
- The Bible
- On Death and Dying, Elisabeth Kübler-Ross
- When Bad Things Happen to Good People, Harold Kushner
- The Gift, Poems by Hafiz
- Reduced to Joy, Mark Nepo

IN CLOSING

It is my hope that this workbook offered some insight, acted as a guide to liberation or helped to encourage you on our own path to recovery.

Being creative can be a great benefit in the healing process, so whether you decided to create your own square-a-day or found a different method to create I would be honored to hear, to see your discoveries. Visit us at www.dswalling.com

EXCERPT FROM THE BOOK

TENDING TO MY WOUNDS
Coping with Grief One Square at a Time

When I dared to look outside the box of my standards, opening my eyes to see and ears to hear beyond my own understanding and expectation I learned to step away from my grief. I began to observe others in their grief and I decided to allow pain and sadness to be my teacher.

I am different now. Those I know, may or may not have noticed; yet I can tell. Grief is no longer painful. Although the sadness of my mother's death will always linger within my heart and soul, with adjustment I was able to regain harmony to and momentum in my life — you can too — in our own way, your own time. The grief, the sadness you experience is yours. Do not feel guilty to treat it and yourself kindly; that may be your deliverance.

.

BLANK PAGES

The following pages are intentionally left blank to be used as a practice area or creating your own Square-a-Day.

Questions or Thoughts?

Visit Us at www.dswalling.com

When you let go of what does not serve you,
you make room for what does.

Author Unknown